Rebecca Manley Pippert
with Dick Molenhouse

EMPOWERED

Equipping everyone for relational evangelism

- LEADER'S GUIDE -

Empowered
Copyright © Rebecca Manley Pippert, 2016
www.beckypippertministries.org

Published by:
The Good Book Company Ltd
Blenheim House, 1 Blenheim Road, Epsom, Surrey, KT19 9AP, UK
Tel: +44 (0) 208 942 0880
Email: info@thegoodbook.com

Published in association with the literary agency of
Wolgemuth & Associates, Inc.

Websites:
North America: www.thegoodbook.com
UK and Europe: www.thegoodbook.co.uk
Australia: www.thegoodbook.com.au
New Zealand: www.thegoodbook.co.nz

ISBN: 9781784981068

Design by André Parker

Printed in Turkey

CONTENTS

WELCOME TO EMPOWERED

I was recently interviewed on an American Christian radio show where people could call in. The subject was evangelism, and ten minutes into the interview the entire phone board lit up with callers from across the country. The comments were revealing.

Every caller spoke of someone they deeply cared about who was not a Christian.

While they longed for their friend to come to Christ, they felt completely inadequate in how to reach them.

Their fears were very similar: How do I raise the topic of faith naturally? What if I offend them or they reject me? What if they raise questions I can't answer?

Everyone essentially asked the same thing: How do I reach people in today's increasingly secular culture? As one caller put it:

"Jesus didn't suggest we share the good news —he commanded us to. But how do we communicate the eternal Christ in our secular, ever-changing world?"

Never has there been a greater need to share Christ with the world (starting with our own neighbors)—yet never have believers seemed more ill-equipped.

And that is why I am thrilled that you are willing to lead others through *Empowered*—a course that equips ordinary Christians for personal evangelism. This leader's guide should contain everything you need to lead effectively.

Empowered has been born through our own experience of helping other Christians to be excited about and equipped for sharing their faith. For the past thirteen years Dick and I have conducted training conferences and have been part of evangelistic initiatives around the world. For the first six years we ministered on every continent (apart from Antarctica!). Then for the next seven, we were focused primarily on Europe. Europe has long been considered the most challenging place for the gospel in the world—yet we have seen amazing fruit as Christians have reached out in even the most unlikely places.

It is imperative that we—all of us—know how to effectively communicate the gospel. We need to get beyond one-size-fits-all techniques. We need to learn to communicate the truth in a way that is also loving. Yet we need to remember, even as we seek to show Christ's compassionate love, still to share Christ's gospel truth.

We need to recover the "Jesus way"—the biblical way—by creatively and persuasively sharing God's truth in the context of authentic relationships and community, so that people may become radical, missional disciples.

Thank you again for giving up your time and energy to lead others through this course. We'll be praying that through your labors, your group and you yourself will be empowered to share the gospel in truth and love. And we'll be praying for your whole group, that the truths you hear, the Bible passages you study, the discussions you have, the thinking you do and the prayers you share will change all of you, and so change the lives and eternities of those around you.

Thanks,

Becky   Dick

HOW TO
RUN THIS COURSE

Empowered is designed to be a flexible course to fit a wide variety of church settings. It can be used:

~ as a seven-week course in midweek groups or Sunday morning adult Sunday School.

~ as the teaching for a church-away day or weekend.

~ for a day conference.

The optimum group size for Bible study and discussion is 6-10—so if your group is larger than this (if, for instance, your whole church is gathered to go through the content), then break into smaller groups, each with one or two leaders.

To run the course, you will need the DVD or downloads... a leader's guide for everyone who will be leading a Bible study or other element of the session... and a handbook for every group member. In this leader's guide, the page numbers in the session-by-session section are the same as the equivalent page numbers in the handbook, to make it easy for you to refer your group to the correct pages.

The elements in every, or almost every, session are:

Intro: A short video clip introducing the theme of the session.

Bible Study: The main Bible input for each session, led by the group leader, allowing God's word to set the agenda for each session.

Talk: Biblically-based, practical presentations, filmed live at a conference in London. Talk outlines are provided in the handbooks and leader's guide.

Talk Notes: Encourage your group to write down, as they listen to the talk, anything they find particularly helpful, need to think more about, or would like to ask a question about. If you have time and find it helpful, you could start the "Discuss" times by asking your group for their own thoughts, questions, etc.

Discuss: A time for you as a group to share your responses to what you have heard, learn from one another, and consider how you might apply the teaching to your lives, guided by the questions given.

Next Steps: Ideas for how group members might begin to live out what they've learned during the session. Give your group time to read through it before you finish with prayer—don't assume they will read it on their own after the session! (Note: If you are running this course over a single day or weekend, the next steps will be impossible to do between each session! So encourage participants to work through the "Next Steps" over the course of seven weeks or so after you have worked through this course.)

Pray: A chance to speak to God together about the themes of the session, either led by Dick via DVD, or done within the group. If the prayer includes DVD footage, see this as an intro to your time of prayer, and continue praying in your group after Dick has led you in prayer on the DVD.

Elements included in some sessions are:

Exercise (Session 5): Introduced by Becky during her talk.

Reflections (Sessions 1 and 7): Opportunities to reflect individually on hopes, questions, applications and resolutions.

TIMINGS

Each session is designed to last 90 minutes, with 15 minutes to enjoy each other's company beforehand. It is, however, possible to fit the session into 60 minutes if necessary. In the grid on page xiv showing the outline of each session, you will find timings for a 75-minute session (not including 15 minutes together before you begin) and a 60-minute session.

EXTRA RESOURCES

During the course, participants will be pointed to extra resources in the back of the handbook which they will need as they follow the "Next Steps." These are:

Praying Powerfully (pages 69-70 of the handbook)—needed for Session 3

Big Questions (pages 71-72)—needed for Sessions 5 and 6

Helpful Ways to Outline the Gospel (pages 73-75)—needed for Session 6

Apologetics: Resources for Answering Tough Questions (page 77)—mentioned by Dick in his Intro to Session 6.

To go alongside Session Seven, you will also find a downloadable Q+A resource, written by Becky, answering common questions about Seeker Bible Studies. Simply go to: thegoodbook.com/SBSAnswers

For advertizing the course beforehand to your church to encourage people to come, you will find promotional material, including a trailer, here: thegoodbook.com/empowered/promo.

LEADING AN EFFECTIVE COURSE

THE BIBLE STUDY AND DISCUSS ELEMENTS

To make the group discussion time as effective as possible, it is important to:

Create an atmosphere of authenticity. Most Christians have fears and a sense of inadequacy when it comes to evangelism (you may well feel that way yourself). Sharing your own failed attempts at witnessing could be an encouragement! But don't be afraid to also share how God has helped you grow stronger in this area. Pray that people will feel free to be themselves.

Create an atmosphere of Christ's love. Christians genuinely want their family members and loved ones to know Christ. But they often feel totally inept at being effective witnesses. So there is usually an amount of guilt and, frankly, a lack of faith that God could use them in their weakness. But as they learn of the transforming power of the gospel—how God loves them and wants to use them just as they are; that he understands their fears and doubts but that the power of witness comes from God, not our giftedness—it will enable them to relax and start believing that they could do this. Pray that each person will experience the love of Christ in a fresh way.

Create interactive participation: One challenge in any group discussion is group dynamics. For example, there is often a talkative person who wants to answer every question. Without diminishing his or her enthusiasm, you could say, "That is helpful. What do the rest of you think?" If the problem persists, then enlist their help outside the study and ask them to help you to draw out the quieter ones. Equally, be ready to ask quieter people for their view by name. Make sure that it is a question that either has a simple answer ("John, what does verse 1 say about how Paul was feeling?"), or one where the answer cannot be wrong ("Evie, what big truth about evangelism are you taking away from this session?").

Don't be afraid of silence: Resist the temptation to answer your own questions! Give people time to reflect on the questions in the Bible study or the Discussion questions. But in your preparation each week, think of alternative ways of asking the same question should there be a prolonged silence.

Beware tangents: These studies are not intended to unpack every aspect of the passage being studied—rather, they focus on what we can learn from the passage about sharing our faith with those around us. They are deliberately limited to 4-5 questions, to ensure you move through the study in the time given in the session. Explain this to your group at the start of the Bible study in Session One, and remind them of it if necessary.

Expect that at some point someone will ask a question that isn't particularly relevant to the topic. For example, when you ask a question on the passage from Luke 23 in Session Two, someone may ask, "Is the casting of lots for Jesus' clothes a fulfillment of Old Testament prophecy?" or "Could the darkness have been an eclipse?" When this happens we need gently but firmly to respond, "Excellent question. But since we have a lot to get through, would you mind if we save it for after the study, or I get back to you about it in the week?" (Be sure you then return to it with that member afterwards!)

Pay attention to time: A critical skill in leading this course is paying attention to the allotted time given to each section. If we allow, for example, the Bible-study discussion to go over, then we will take away from the other important aspects of this course. While we don't want to appear to be drill sergeants, it is very important to keep each section roughly in the allotted time.

THE IMPORTANCE OF PRAYER

Pray each week at home for the people in your group.

Pray for their faith to grow and that they'll develop confidence that God can use them.

Ask God for fruit! "This is to my Father's glory, that you bear much fruit, showing yourselves to be my disciples" (John 15 v 8). Pray that God will lead the participants during the course to non-Christians who are, or will quickly become, spiritually open, and that they'll have encouraging conversations.

Pray that there will be conversions. Just one person leading a seeker to Christ will have a huge impact on the whole group!

Give time for prayer in your group.

Encourage each person to pray. Acknowledge that praying aloud in front of others can be awkward at first. Encourage those who are anxious about it to just attempt short, one-sentence prayers until they feel more comfortable. Eventually this will be something they really look forward to.

PRAYER PARTNERS

Encourage your group in the first week to select a "prayer partner" from within the group to meet with once a week for the duration of the course (if you are doing the course in a day or over a weekend, then the prayer partners would meet for the next few weeks, as participants work through the "Next Steps" week by week). This will enable them to pray and discuss what they are learning, and to follow through on the "Next Steps"—and it will dramatically help them to apply what they are learning. The temptation in modern culture is to be a consumer: we are willing to receive but not to act upon the truth we are learning. Having a prayer partner strengthens us in actually getting on with living out what we've learned and have been equipped for and challenged about.

SESSION OUTLINES

Note: If you are using this course on a weekend away or at a day conference, you need only use Intro One and can skip the rest of the Intros. You can also use the Talks without the Bible Studies if this best suits your requirements and timetable.

SESSION		NORMAL SESSION	60-MINUTE OPTION
1. Inadequacy is Compulsory	Reflection: Before you begin...	5 mins	3
	Intro (DVD)	4	4
	Bible Study: 1 Corinthians 2 v 1-5	10	8
	Talk (DVD)	35	35
	Discuss	15	5
	Pray (DVD)	6	5
2. The Cross: The Mess and the Miracle	Intro (DVD)	3	3
	Bible Study: Luke 23 v 32-49	17	12
	Talk (DVD)	30	30
	Discuss	20	10
	Pray (DVD)	5	5
3. Facing our Fears	Intro (DVD)	3	3
	Bible Study: Joshua 1 v 1-11	15	10
	Talk & Exercise (DVD)	40	35
	Discuss	7	7
	Pray	10	5
4. It's All about Relationships	Intro (DVD)	5	5
	Bible Study: Luke 19 v 1-10	15	10
	Talk (DVD)	30	30
	Discuss	15	10
	Pray	10	5

SESSION		NORMAL SESSION	60-MINUTE OPTION
5. Cultivating Curiosity	Intro (DVD)	4	4
	Bible Study: John 4 v 5-30	17	10
	Talk (DVD)	34	34
	Exercise	15	7
	Pray	5	5
6. The Gospel: Content and Response	Intro (DVD)	4	4
	Bible Study: Acts 2 v 14-41	16	11
	Talk One (DVD)	15	15
	Discuss	15	8
	Talk Two (DVD)	17	17
	Pray	8	5
7. Introducing the Irresistible Jesus	Intro (DVD)	5	5
	Talk (DVD)	30	30
	How Not to Lead a Seeker Bible Study (DVD)	8	5
	Bible Study: Luke 5 v 17-26	15	10
	Goodbye! (DVD)	7	7
	Reflection: As you finish...	5	3
	Pray	5	0

THE COURSE:
SESSION BY SESSION

INADEQUACY
IS COMPULSORY

REFLECTION: AS YOU BEGIN...

What three words best describe how you feel about evangelism?

What do you hope to get out of doing this course?

INTRO

BIBLE STUDY

Read 1 Corinthians 2 v 1-5

1. How did Paul feel about sharing the gospel with people in Corinth?

    Verse 3: Weak and fearful. Paul was "trembling."

2. What did he focus on talking about? Why, do you think?

    Presumably, Paul understood that the central "testimony about God"—the core of his message and the place where he has most clearly spoken about himself—is in Jesus, and at the cross of Jesus. So the one thing the Corinthians needed to hear about, in order to understand who God is and how they could relate to him, was Jesus Christ and his death on the cross.

3. What did Paul's message not come with, and what did accompany it (v 4-5)?

> It did not come with "wise and persuasive words"—it did come with " a demonstration of the Spirit's power" (this likely refers to the way the message was received—the Spirit's power was shown in people responding in faith). The city of Corinth greatly prized rhetorical ability ("wise and persuasive words")—but Paul did not seek to win prizes for oratory. He simply sought to declare the truth about Jesus.

Why was that a good thing for the faith of the people who did listen to him?

> If the Corinthians had put their faith in Jesus because they were impressed by Paul, then their faith would "rest on human wisdom" (v 5). So if someone else who sounded wiser came along, their faith would crumble; or if Paul left Corinth, they would be left without the foundation of their faith. But their faith was not founded on Paul or his wisdom, but "on God's power" through his Spirit—and that could not be surpassed, and would never leave.

4. When we feel weak about talking to others about Jesus, how is Paul both an encouragement and a challenge to us?

> It is encouraging to see that even such a great evangelist as the apostle Paul felt weak, fearful and trembling at the prospect of sharing the gospel with non-Christians—just as we so often do! It is not wrong to feel this way. But it is therefore very challenging to realize that Paul felt this way, and witnessed anyway. It means that weakness and trembling is not an excuse for not speaking about Jesus.

TALK

1. Our Motivation for Witness—God the Father

Jesus was criticized for mingling with sinners, and responded by telling three stories (Luke 15):

~ The Lost Sheep

~ The Lost Coin

~ Two Lost Sons

God searches for the lost and rejoices when they are found. He loves people, and so must we.

2. Our Model for Witness—Jesus

The eternal Son of God came to live on earth as a weak human being!

God's glory and power is revealed through human weakness (1 Corinthians 2 v 3-5).

Jesus' life reveals what it means to be human—we are created to be God-dependent people, not self-sufficient people.

Our feelings of inadequacy remind us that we are not God; but celebrating our smallness frees us to depend on God's power.

3. Our Means for Witness—the Holy Spirit

We depend on God's power by "remaining" in Christ (John 15)—he dwells within us through the Holy Spirit.

The "Three Rs":

~ *Remember* in every situation that Jesus is with us.

~ *Rejoice* that we have access to God's power through Christ (Matthew 28 v 20).

~ *Request* the Lord's help in every situation.

God has always used the weak to accomplish his purposes—he can use you too.

TALK NOTES

DISCUSS

1. "God has always used the weak to accomplish his purposes." How have you witnessed this, in your own experience or in those you know? When do you find it hardest to believe the truth of this, and why?

2. How do you respond to the idea that inadequacy is not an obstacle to evangelism—it's a necessity?

3. Remember... Rejoice... Request. How could you start, or keep, consciously practicing the presence of Christ this week? What do you think might change if you do that?

4. What is the one big truth from this session that you will apply to your attitude to evangelism?

NEXT STEPS

~ Between now and the next session, consciously practice the presence of Christ, abiding in him by remembering, rejoicing and requesting.

~ If you're able to, arrange to meet another member of your group this week to pray together (from now on, we'll call this person your "prayer partner").

~ Either with your prayer partner, and/or each day on your own, ask God to grant you both a deeper faith and greater awareness of his power and presence.

 PRAY

2

THE CROSS:
THE MESS AND THE MIRACLE

INTRO

BIBLE STUDY

Read Luke 23 v 32-49

1. From verses 33-49, Jesus is hanging on a cross—the one who had claimed to be a king is being killed as a criminal. What responses to him does Luke show us?

> **Observing (v 35):** The watching people appear to have observed, but not to have made any response or allowed what they saw to affect them.
> **Sneering and mockery (v 35):** The rulers and soldiers argued that if Jesus really were God's almighty King, he would save himself and get off his cross. Since he didn't, he couldn't be the Christ.

Insults (v 39): Even a dying criminal chooses to use some of his last words to mock Jesus and his claims.

Humble request (v 40-42): The other dying criminal accepts that he is facing death and God's judgment "justly," but recognizes that Jesus is innocent. And he asks Jesus to "remember me" (to help him and act on his behalf) when he comes into his kingdom. This criminal seems to understand that Jesus truly is God's King, that he will rule a kingdom beyond death, and that he has the power to bring others into that kingdom.

Recognition (v 47): A hardened Roman soldier realizes that "this was a righteous man"—that Jesus is not a guilty criminal, but an innocent, godly man. Mark records the centurion saying that "this man was the Son of God" (Mark 15 v 39)—so this appears to be a confession of faith.

2. Which of those responses to Jesus' death do you see around you today?

> Your group will likely see all these responses. Many glance at the cross but it makes no difference to them; some merely mock the whole idea that God would send his Son to die, or would like to tell Jesus that if he really is God, then he would sort out their problems; others recognize who Jesus is and what he died on the cross to offer, and ask for a place in eternity with him.

3. What do Jesus' words (each of which would have been agony to utter) show us about his character?

> "Father, forgive them, for they do not know what they are doing" (v 34)—what compassion, to pray for those who are executing him. Jesus' great hope, even for his enemies, is that they would confess their sins (including those they had not even realized they were committing) and find forgiveness from God.
>
> "Truly I tell you, today you will be with me in paradise" (v 43)—Jesus welcomes sinners into his eternal kingdom. He does reign, and he does have the ability to welcome others in, however they have lived their lives.
>
> "Father, into your hands I commit my spirit" (v 46). Jesus was trusting and humble even in his weakness and his death. He had confidence that his Father would see him through death.

4. *Read 1 Peter 3 v 18.* How could Jesus offer the most lawbreaking man in this scene—a condemned criminal dying at his side—a place "with me in paradise" (Luke 23 v 42)?

> Because he was dying in his place. Jesus was righteous—innocent and perfect in God's sight—but he died "for"—instead of, or on behalf of—the "unrighteous"—those like this criminal who had sinned. And the achievement of his death in this criminal's place was that Jesus took his judgment—bore his separation from God—so that this sinner could be brought "to God."

5. How does the cross turn upside down the assumptions this world makes about who is powerful... who is good... who needs help... who has eternal life?

> The most powerful one in this scene is nailed to a cross! The most righteous man in this scene is killed as a criminal, while religious leaders—"good" people—laugh at him. Everyone needs help, though they do not all realize it. And by the end of the day, a dead criminal is enjoying eternal life while religious leaders are missing out on it.

TALK

Jesus makes a real difference. But we can't benefit from the cure that Christ brings unless we face the problem—sin (Jeremiah 17 v 9).

Secular culture—and often even our church culture—denies that sin is the problem.

Jesus Died and We Crucified Him (Acts 2 v 23)

All of us are responsible for the death of the only innocent One—so our capacity for sin shouldn't surprise us.

The cross shows us that whatever we have done can be forgiven—because God is willing to forgive us even for the death of Christ.

Jesus Died and We were Crucified with Him (Galatians 2 v 19-20)

On the cross Jesus bore our sin, and our old self was nailed to the cross with him.

We have a new identity—sin no longer defines us.

Walking in the Light of the Cross

We identify and confess our sin.

We are free to love the unlovely, because we suffer from the same disease and need the same cure.

All is grace: remember that no one is beyond the reach of our wonderful Savior.

TALK NOTES

DISCUSS

1. Would a newcomer to your church get the impression that everyone there was a sinner in need of forgiveness, or a good person whose life was sorted? What can you do, as a group or individuals, to make clear that as Christians, you admit the problem as well as offering the answer?

2. How does the "god-complex" display itself in your life?

3. Is there someone you struggle to love, or think is beyond the reach of Christ's forgiveness? How has reflecting on the cross in this situation changed or challenged your attitude?

4. "Jesus died and we crucified him. Never underestimate sin when it cost Jesus his life. But Jesus died and we were crucified with him. Don't overestimate sin either. You're freer than you know."
   What difference will it make to you neither to under- nor overestimate your sin this week?

NEXT STEPS

~ Practice explaining why Jesus died on the cross. Aim not to use any words or phrases that someone who has never been to church wouldn't have heard before. And aim to explain it in a single minute.
If you can, practice with another member of your group, or a friend from church.
Even better... ask a non-Christian friend, family member or co-worker if they would mind you practicing with them! You may feel inadequate, but that's OK!

~ As you pray over the next few days, ask God to show you three or four non-Christians with whom he would like you to share the gospel. Once you have identified those people, commit to praying for them each day.

PRAY

3

FACING OUR FEARS

 INTRO

BIBLE STUDY

Read Joshua 1 v 1-11

God calls Joshua to do something very challenging that will lead to testing, conflict, struggles and pressure. But first God calls and commissions Joshua.

1. How would it help Joshua in his future challenges to know that God had clearly revealed to him his will and pleasure (v 1-4)?

> The task was huge—Israel were to "cross the River Jordan" (v 2) and settle in a massive area (v 4). To this point, Israel had never owned a land. Now they had to fight for one. So God reminds Joshua that this is all part of his plans: "I will give you every place where you set your foot, as I promised Moses" (v 3). When Joshua faces problems and setbacks, he can know that God's will is to give this land to his people.

2. After revealing his will, what qualities does God say Joshua needs in order to obey God's purposes (v 5-9)?

> He will need to be strong and courageous (v 6, 7, 9), and to avoid terror or discouragement (v 9). He will also need to be obedient to God's law and commands (v 7, 8).

How do we obtain these qualities?

> The same way Joshua did. By remembering that God is with us (v 5); by knowing, treasuring, relying on and following God's "law" as we find it in his word (v 8); and by relying on his promises (v 6). We find strength and courage not from within, but by remembering the presence of God with us, by reading the word of God to us, and by relying on the promises of God for us.

Clearly, moral strength and courage are increased by knowing God's will and word, and by trusting God's promises.

3. *Read Matthew 28 v 18-20.* What similar commands and promise does Jesus make to his people here, compared to God's words to Joshua?

> Joshua is told to go over the Jordan to settle the land. The disciples are told to "go" to all the nations to make disciples of them. Both seem almost impossible tasks!
> Joshua is told to obey God's law—the disciples are told to teach everyone to obey all that Jesus commanded them.
> Joshua is promised the presence of God with him; and Jesus promises his people that "surely I am with you always, to the very end of the age."

4. God knew Joshua would experience fear as he sought to obey God's commands. That is also true for us. We need to be obedient to God and yet realistic about life's challenges. What fears might take hold of us when we share our faith?

> Allow your group to make suggestions based on their own personal experience.
> There is no need to let this discussion go on too long, since the subject of the talk and discussion is how to face and deal with our fears about evangelism.

What have we learned about what to do when we are afraid?

> We need to remember that Jesus is with us.
> We need to remember that Jesus has sent us to be part of his plans for his world by witnessing to his world.
> We need to remember God's word and get on with obeying it, even when that is hard.

TALK

The drive to evangelism is a fire within. So...

What Diminishes our Fire?

1. Complacency

Perhaps all our friends are Christians, or we're busy.

2. Confusion

~ Over how to tell the gospel (with our lips and lives)

~ Over who's meant to tell the gospel (Matthew 28 v 19 implies that it is all of us!)

~ Over God's role and our role. God opens eyes and hearts (2 Corinthians 4 v 6; Acts 16 v 14). We are to speak the message and invite people to respond.

3. Fears

Write down your three biggest fears when it comes to evangelism:

1.

2.

3.

The Fear of Offending

~ Be authentic—tell your friend you're worried about offending.

~ Develop a style consistent with your personality.

The Fear of Being Rejected

~ Fear is normal, but we must obey despite our fear (Acts 18 v 9)

The Fear of Not Knowing Answers to Questions

~ Affirm the question, ask about background and admit your ignorance if necessary!

The Fear of Inconsistencies

~ We're not perfect—but we don't need to be.

Our Hidden Fear: What if God doesn't come through?

~ Our fears all focus on ourselves; our biggest need is the Spirit's power—God-confidence, not self-confidence.

~ Our problem is the sin of unbelief—we must trust that God goes before us.

TALK NOTES

DISCUSS

1. Having heard Becky's talk and thought about your fears, what would you now say are the three fears or factors most likely to stop you talking about Jesus with someone?

2. What have you learned that will help you when you feel afraid?

NEXT STEPS

~ Commit to praying frequently, daily, for the people you think Christ is calling you to share his gospel with.

~ Continue to pray that God will make you a winsome witness. (Look at the "Praying Powerfully" section on pages 29-30 for help in how to pray).

~ Invite one of the people you are praying for to do something this week—it could be as simple as getting a cup of coffee. If the topic of faith naturally arises (and pray it will!), then great. But take this time to build the friendship and to get to know each other better. Aim to gently ask questions about their family background and discover what their interests are.

~ As your friendship deepens, try to discover what questions they have about God. What seem to be their resistant points to Christianity?

Note: It may be that, for one reason or another, you need to move through these "Next Steps" more slowly than getting each done between each session. That's fine (as long as it's not just an excuse!). If you need to, move through each set of "Next Steps" at your own pace, so that you'll finish them some time after the course itself finishes.

PRAY

Use these suggestions to pray together as you finish the session, and to include in your prayers on your own this coming week.

~ Confess your fears and areas of unbelief that block you from trusting God's power; ask the Lord to enable you to trust that he desires to use you just as you are.

~ Ask God to reveal the people in your life who are spiritually open; and to help you to develop genuine friendships and start having easy, lively spiritual discussion.

~ Ask God for greater faith in his power and greater dependence on his Spirit; and ask him to make you an effective witness.

4

IT'S ALL ABOUT RELATIONSHIPS

INTRO

BIBLE STUDY

Read Luke 19 v 1-10

Tax collectors worked for the occupying Roman authorities, and they became rich by over-charging their countrymen and keeping the difference for themselves. Unsurprisingly, Jews hated them.

1. So what is surprising about Jesus' treatment of this wealthy tax collector?

> Jesus chooses to speak to Zacchaeus—not only that, he insists on staying at his house (v 5). In a culture where eating together and extending hospitality played a crucial role in showing friendship and acceptance, Jesus is saying, *I am going to be friends with you and associated with you.* Jesus wants to be friends with this man who has given up all right to be accepted or liked.

2. Why is the crowd's horrified reaction in verse 7 entirely understandable?

> The people watching "mutter" about Jesus' decision to attend the house of a "sinner." They're incredulous at Jesus' choice. And that's understandable—this man has betrayed God's ancient people, ignored God, and given up his principles for money. How could God's Son choose to spend time with him? Why would he want to? Zacchaeus is the least deserving of all of them—yet Jesus wants to eat at his house.

3. How does Jesus explain why he has treated Zacchaeus as he has (v 9-10)?

> Jesus came to bring "salvation" (v 9). He—the "Son of Man"—"came to seek and to save the lost." Zacchaeus was certainly lost—lost in the consequences of the sinful decisions he had made. And Jesus looked for him, and welcomed him, and would go on to Jerusalem to die for him. Zacchaeus is not the most unlikely person for Jesus to choose to befriend—he is exactly the kind of person Jesus came to seek and save.

4. What difference does Jesus make to Zacchaeus (v 5-6, 8)?

> Zacchaeus "welcomed [Jesus] gladly" (v 6). There is a new joy in his life, brought about by being friends with Jesus.
> Zacchaeus completely changed his view of money. He had given up a great deal to become wealthy; now he gives away a large part of that wealth. He does not merely give back what he owes, but more than that. Knowing Jesus and his friendship means that Zacchaeus now gives away generously what he had once greedily grasped onto. His heart and his priorities have changed.

5. Imagine that "the people" in verse 7 were actually taking this course with you. What might be their attitude toward reaching out to others?

> There would likely be some "types" of people around them who they did not truly want to reach out to, especially if it involved making an effort to do so. Deep down, they would see some people as too undeserving of Jesus' love, or too unlikely to accept Jesus' offer, and therefore not worth building real relationships with.

What would Zacchaeus say if he were taking this course a few weeks after meeting Jesus?

> He would surely understand, given his own testimony, that no one is beyond Jesus' love or reach. He would also know that he was no better than anyone else, and was included in God's people only because Jesus had chosen to invite him in. So he wouldn't look down on anyone around him. (As a side point, verse 8 suggests that he'd be happy to use his money to support mission.)

TALK

Building authentic relationships with unbelievers is key to evangelism.

The story of the Good Samaritan gives us some profound principles for evangelism (Luke 10 v 25-37).

1. The Kingdom of God is Relational

Jesus sums up life in terms of love relationships—with God and our neighbor.

God didn't hand out flyers to the world—he sent his Son.

God is triune—a relational being.

2. Jesus Radically Identified with People

Jesus had a "go to them"—not "come to us"—approach.

Jesus understood our human experience from the inside out—we must seek to understand our friends' doubts, questions and pain.

Jesus demonstrated that everybody is somebody to God.

Are you involved in authentic friendships where you share your life with unbelieving friends?

3. Jesus was Radically Different—we should be too. How?

We display God's love with our actions.

We depend on God's power through prayer.

We declare God's truth by presenting people with the real Jesus of the Bible—he's irresistible!

TALK NOTES

DISCUSS

1. Do you think that, by character, you tend more towards being radically identified with the world, or radically different? How does Jesus' example help you to be both?

2. "Jesus never treated people as merely evangelistic projects. He established real relationships with real people."
What stops us establishing real relationships with non-Christians?

3. Imagine someone spent a month living in your house and going with you to your church (on Sundays and any other church activities). From looking at you and your church, what would they conclude matters most to Jesus?

4. Why is it liberating to realize that Jesus calls us to have real friendships with people, rather than to stand aloof, or run in, hit someone with the gospel, and run off again? Are there any changes you need to make in your schedule in order to pursue real, natural relationships with these people?

NEXT STEPS

~ Identify (or discuss with your prayer partner) the chief interests of the people you are praying for: music, art, sports, films, food? Again, as the relationship develops, try to understand where they are spiritually. Are they spiritually open, closed, interested, hostile or bored? And why? What do they not understand about Christianity?

~ Then plan a casual social activity that you, your prayer partner and at least two seekers could do in the next two weeks. It doesn't matter that they don't know each other. Just invite them to do something they'd like—and then perhaps suggest a meal afterwards. Use the time to get to know each other and have fun! Pray that the topic of faith might come up—but don't push it. One question your friends will probably ask is how you and your Christian friend know each other—and you can casually say, "Oh, we go to the same church" (or something similar).

PRAY

~ Ask God to help you understand the needs and questions in the lives of your friends, and to give you a deeper experience and conviction of his love for them.

~ Ask God to create in your friends a curiosity about Jesus and a hunger for meaning and purpose.

~ Pray that your friends will see something in your life that draws them to God.

5

CULTIVATING
CURIOSITY

INTRO

BIBLE STUDY

Read John 4 v 5-30

To understand how Jesus sparked this woman's curiosity, it is important to know that in Jesus' day Jews and Samaritans hated each other. Furthermore, men and women never spoke to each other in public. And religious leaders would be risking their reputation if they spoke publicly to a woman—especially one who (as we learn in verse 18) had been married five times and was now living with a man who wasn't her husband.

1. What does Jesus do that astonishes this Samaritan woman and gets her attention (v 7-9)?

> He asks her for a drink (v 7). This is astonishing not because of the request, but because of who is making it, and to whom. He is a Jewish man (and a teacher with a following)—she is a Samaritan woman. This is what the woman points out in verse 9. Jesus has certainly surprised her!

What does it tell us about Jesus that he initiates a conversation with this woman when he is tired, thirsty and hungry?

> As with Zacchaeus in the last session, we see that Jesus wanted to speak with and offer friendship to those on the outside of society. And here, we see his commitment to this in the fact that he makes the effort to reach out to this woman even though he is tired, thirsty and hungry. He does not use his fatigue as an excuse for not bothering with her.

2. What does Jesus say in verses 10 and 13-14 that cultivates her curiosity? Do you think the woman understands what Jesus is offering (v 15)?

> Verse 10: He suggests that he has a kind of water that she won't find in the well—"living water." And he also suggests that she does not know who he is—he is no mere "Jew" (v 9).
> Verse 13: Jesus contrasts the water in the well with his living water. The former quenches thirst for a while, but its effects wear off and more water will be needed. But his water quenches thirst forever—and it brings eternal life.
> But it seems that she does not understand the offer. She thinks Jesus is talking about real water—so she hopes to be given some so that she doesn't need to return to the well.

Then, just when the woman asks for this living water, Jesus suddenly delves into her personal life and asks her to go call her husband.

3. Why do you think Jesus wants her to see that her sin is the reason that she needs what he is offering?

> The thing his "water" will replace is not her repeated trips to the "well" with her many relationships with men (which clearly left her empty and unsatisfied), but her relationship to the true God. Jesus brings up her moral past in order to help her see that in her search for fulfillment and love, they can't be found in sinful relationships with men – but in a heartfelt, obedient and loving relationship with God.

If Jesus had given her the "living water" when she first asked for it, she wouldn't have understood what it was and why she needed it. He didn't manipulate her into a premature decision.
When the disciples saw Jesus talking with this woman, they were astonished. They couldn't see what he saw: this woman wasn't a lost cause to God. She had been trying to meet her needs in all the wrong places. Her lifestyle revealed that she was thirsty for God!

4. What lessons and encouragements can we learn for our evangelism from this story?

> Guide your group to come up with some of these answers (they may, of course, also offer others): We don't look at a sinful person and keep our distance—we look deeper and ask what is revealed about their need for God.
> We learn never to assume that even the most unlikely-looking person would not be open to the gospel—because a sinful lifestyle might be the very indicator that this person is thirsty for God without realizing it.
> We learn from Jesus the importance of rousing curiosity.
> We learn to affirm the good we see in someone, no matter how troubled their life (notice that Jesus encourages her twice in verse 17 for telling him the truth that she has no husband—"you are right ... what you have just said is quite true").
> We don't drop a friendship with a non-Christian just because other Christians may not approve.
> We don't allow tiredness to get in the way of God-given opportunities to talk about Jesus.

TALK

1. There is a Process Involved in Evangelism

We cultivate curiosity.

We share the message.

We invite a response.

2. How do we Cultivate Curiosity in the Gospel?

We Cultivate Curiosity by Depending on God's Power (1 Corinthians 4 v 20).

- ~ Pray for yourself—for God's power and authority.

- ~ Pray for your friend—in specific, intelligent ways.

- ~ Pray with your friend—if they share a problem, ask whether they would mind you praying for them right then.

We Cultivate Curiosity through Sharing Truth

- ~ Investigate: ask gentle questions to understand their barriers to faith.

- ~ Stimulate their interest (like Jesus with the Samaritan woman in John 4) by addressing their barriers to faith.

We Cultivate Curiosity through Showing God's Love

3. Raise the Topic of Faith by Asking Good Questions

General interest questions

Specific interest questions (What? Why? How?)

Issue questions—that cause them to reflect on what they believe

"God" questions

TALK NOTES

EXERCISE

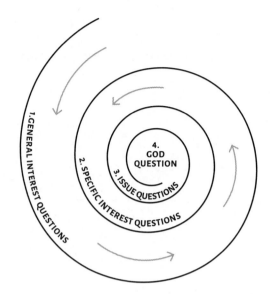

Name:

Interest:

Questions:

1.

2.

3.

4.

NEXT STEPS

~ Work out some areas of interest about which you could chat with a friend (or friends), and work out some questions you could ask that will help you move from general to "issue" or "God" questions. Then go ask them the questions!
Aim to have at least one conversation this week in which you move to asking an "Issue" or even a "God" question. It may seem stilted or awkward at first, but over time you'll get more adept at connecting people's interests and passions with larger issues and even with their consideration of God. Remember, practice makes perfect (or at least proficient!).

~ This week, seek to ask at least one of the people you are praying for the "Big Questions" (you'll find the questions on pages 71-72.) You could say, "I heard a speaker at a course we're doing at church say that Christians need to do a better job of listening to and understanding what their friends believe. She gave us some thought-provoking questions to ask our friends. Would you be willing to get a cup of coffee and tell me what you think? I'd be really interested to find out!"
If they say "Yes" (and most do), then meet twice, over the next couple of weeks, to cover the questions. It's fine to have the questions written on a piece of paper—but don't take notes on their answers! Listen actively, and if you need them to explain further, then say so. Don't offer your opinion unless they ask. This might seem intimidating at first—but people almost universally say they loved the experience. Remember to conclude by saying how much you've enjoyed listening to what they think. Ask if you could meet one more time next week to ask their opinion of some other questions!

PRAY

~ Ask God to use you to prompt curiosity about Christian faith in your friends.

~ Ask God to guide you to the right person (or people) of whom to ask the "Big Questions," and for courage to speak to them about it; and that these conversations will lead to fruitful, positive discussion about the gospel.

~ Pray that you (and your prayer partner if you have one) would be able to gather for a social time together with some friends with whom you feel the Lord is leading you to share more of your life and the gospel.

6

THE GOSPEL:
CONTENT AND RESPONSE

 INTRO

BIBLE STUDY

Read Acts 2 v 22-41

1. What does Peter say in verses 22-24 about:

~ Jesus' life?

Jesus of Nazareth—a real man, with a name and a hometown—was "accredited by God" (v 22)—that is, his identity was revealed by God. His life—his "miracles, wonders and signs"—were signs of who he was.

~ Jesus' death?

He died as a result of "God's deliberate plan and foreknowledge" (v 23)—Jesus' death was not an accident, but part of a divine plan. Yet at the same time, people "put him to death"—Jesus' death was also the decision of people to reject his identity and rule, and execute him instead of worshiping him.

~ Jesus' resurrection?

He was raised by God (v 24) because "it was impossible for death to keep its hold on him." Everyone else is powerless before death. But Jesus was so powerful that he had to triumph over death, which is powerless before him.

2. How does he challenge the people (v 23, 36)?

Peter tells them that they were responsible for his death (v 23, 36). And that is a problem because, whereas their verdict on this man was to reject and crucify him, God's verdict is that he is "both Lord and Messiah"—that is, that he is divine ("Lord") and the all-powerful, eternal King whom God had promised to send ("Messiah", or "Christ"). Peter does not hold back! He says to his listeners, *You have killed God's Son, your King. You killed him, and now he is alive again...*

How do they react to the news that this Jesus is "both Lord and Messiah"—both God, and the promised King (v 36-37)?

They are "cut to the heart," because they realize they have killed the now ever-reigning King. They tremble because of their sin against him. And they ask if there is anything they can do.

3. What does Peter call them to do in response to the news that Jesus is the risen Lord and Messiah (v 38-40)?

> They need to do two things: *repent*—which means to turn their lives around completely, so that they no longer seek to be in charge and reject Jesus as King, but instead they now accept he is in charge, and they worship and obey him; and *be baptized*—a way of making a public declaration of this new allegiance.
> And this accepting of Jesus as their King will have two results: *forgiveness*—they are sinners, seen most clearly in their killing of Jesus, but their King is offering them forgiveness; and *the gift of the Holy Spirit*—the Spirit of Jesus will dwell with them.

4. What are the three essential points of the gospel that we see in verses 22-24?

> Jesus was a man who, through his deeds, showed that he was God's unique messenger.
> Jesus died on the cross as a result of human rejection of his claims, but also as part of God's plan and purpose.
> Jesus was raised back to life, because he is more powerful than death. He is alive now.

5. Peter was talking to Jews who had been in Jerusalem at the time of Jesus' death. The people we talk to are in a very different situation! How would you say the same truths as Peter, and make the same call as Peter, in a way that would connect with those who live and work around you?

> This is an opportunity for your group to think about how they would communicate the same message in a way that can be understood by and seem attractive to those who live around you (which will vary depending on your setting and the make-up of your particular group). The important thing to clarify is that we must not change or miss out any of the truths about Jesus' life, death and resurrection—nor may we change the call, which is still to admit we have been living the wrong way, and turn to accept Jesus as King so that we can be forgiven and enjoy his presence. The way we communicate this will be different, but the truths themselves must remain the same.
> For instance, those we speak to did not kill Jesus in Jerusalem 2,000 years ago. But they have rejected Jesus' rule, and lived as though he were not the King. They, like we and like Peter's hearers, are sinners. So the central truth that we need to communicate is the same, though we will do so in a different way (and, in some contexts and with some people today, we might not mention the word "sin", just as Peter did not).

TALK ONE

Loving people is important but it's not enough—we need to speak truth.

The gospel can transform lives because it's authored by Christ himself (Galatians 1 v 11-12). It's profound but can be communicated simply.

One outline of the gospel:

1. Creator: The way life was meant to be

God created us to live in intimacy, love and harmony with him and everyone else.

2. Crisis: The mess we made of things

Life on this planet is full of brokenness and suffering.

The first humans rebelled and chose self-rule—and we've done the same.

God's fair but painful judgment is that we suffer the consequences of our sin—in this life and the next.

3. Christ: The cure

On the cross, Jesus took the judgment we deserve.

He was raised to life to offer us a new, dynamic relationship with God.

4. Commitment: God's offer and our response

God offers to forgive all our sins and give us the Holy Spirit.

We must respond to the offer.

5. Completion: The future

One day Jesus will return and make all things new. His people will enjoy God's perfect presence forever.

TALK NOTES

DISCUSS

1. There are many ways to explain the truth of the gospel, including the way Peter did it in Acts 2, and the way Becky communicated it in her talk. There are a few other ideas on pages 73-75 of this book.
   Look through them now in pairs. Then take it in turns to explain the gospel to each other clearly and warmly in a single minute. Tell each other what you each did well, and what you could work on.

2. Dick said in his introduction that one of the tools we need is our testimony—how God worked in us to bring us to faith. Using these "headings," briefly explain to each other your story of faith:

   ~ What life was like before you knew Christ

   ~ The circumstances and/or people God used to start to open your eyes

   ~ How you came into a relationship with Christ

   ~ How Christ has affected your life since then

▷TALK TWO

God's intention is to transform us. Jesus offers abundant life (John 10 v 10) but warns us to count the cost of following him (Luke 14 v 25-35).

Transformation comes from conversion. Conversion is a mystery!

Our Role...

Watch for the movement of the Spirit.

Speak. Ask, "Is there any reason why you couldn't become a Christian right now?"

Listen to their answer and address any issues they raise.

What is Involved in Making a Commitment to Christ?

The human side: Believing... Repenting... Receiving...

The divine side: Forgiveness of sins and the gift of the Holy Spirit

So someone needs to say:

~ I believe.

~ I am sorry.

~ Come into my life, Jesus.

TALK NOTES

NEXT STEPS

~ If you feel that you need more practice, then share the gospel and your conversion story with your prayer partner. Give each other feedback on where you are strong and what you need to work on.

~ Aim to get together to ask your friend the second set of "Big Questions" (see pages 71-72).

~ Ask God to give you an opportunity to share the gospel message with someone this week (it may be with the person to whom you've been asking the questions, or someone totally unexpected!). Pray that you'll explain it in a way that is faithful, clear and compelling.

PRAY

~ Ask God to give you a real understanding and love for the gospel—and the confidence and skill to communicate it clearly.

~ Spend time now praising God for the amazing good news of his Son, the Lord Jesus Christ.

~ If you asked a friend the "Big Questions" between the last session and this one, pray that your friend will want to continue by answering the second group of questions, and that you will have the opportunity to share the gospel. If you didn't manage to invite a friend to talk through the first set of questions, pray for an opportunity and courage to do so.

7

INTRODUCING
THE IRRESISTIBLE JESUS

INTRO

TALK

Jesus is beautiful, radical and controversial! Introduce unbelieving friends to him through a Seeker Bible Study (SBS).

What is a Seeker Bible Study?

A Bible study for anyone with little or no understanding about Christianity, looking at Jesus, where people discover the answers directly from the Bible text.

Why is a Seeker Bible Study Effective?

Most people don't have a clue who Jesus is.

No one has to believe anything in order to come. They can investigate for themselves.

A S.A.F.E. P.L.A.C.E.

~ **S**afe—everyone is accepted

~ **A**uthenticity—they can be who they really are

~ **F**ood and **F**un!

~ **E**veryday language—don't use "God-talk"

~ **P**rocess not pressure; **P**rayer (but not at the start of the study)

~ **L**ove of Christ and **L**ow-key

~ **A**mazed by the relevance of the Bible

~ **C**are for them pastorally—meet up one-to-one

~ **E**veryone is welcome

What are the Advantages for Believers?

You are not posing as the authority, and you don't have to be gifted in evangelism.

Your faith will grow.

Any positive response is positive!

Before leading a study, think through who, what size, where and when.

Inviting people:

~ Pray!

~ "Have you ever, as an adult, read one of the biographies of Jesus?"

~ Suggest getting together just once to start with.

~ Make clear they don't need to believe the Bible is historically reliable.

The first meeting:

~ Chat and have nibbles and drinks to start

~ You could use an SBS guide

~ Review the purpose of the group

~ At the end, invite people to continue.

TALK NOTES

▷ HOW NOT TO LEAD A SEEKER BIBLE STUDY

Write down everything the co-leaders of this group get *wrong*:

> *There are many, many! Your group may get a different list than this, but here is my list...*
>
> *Praying in front of the group before you begin*
>
> *How you talk about non-Christians: "unbelieving friends," "unsaved neighbors"*
>
> *Using jargon: word of God, justified, sanctified, washed in the blood of the Lamb, Amen*
>
> *Not giving a page number with the Bible reference or helping in some other way to find John 4 v 5*
>
> *Laughing at people's struggles or misunderstandings (about the NIV translation, and where John is in the Bible)*
>
> *Impatience with group members*
>
> *Not knowing a group member's name*
>
> *Response: to people's answers: patronizing, critical, or horrified*
>
> *Asking questions that cannot be answered from the Bible text or from general experience of life*

You could finish by asking your group to think through what it would have looked like if the co-leaders had got it "right" in each of those moments.

BIBLE STUDY

Note: On the next three pages is a cut-down version of the first study in *Uncovering the Life of Jesus*, a Seeker Bible Study. Your group will need to move through the study considerably more quickly than a group of non-Christians who were doing this study "properly" would. Encourage short answers and discourage tangents! The purpose is for each of you to see what a "Seeker Bible Study" is like. You'll find answers to the questions on pages 62-63.

LUKE 5 v 17-26

Standing room only

Question

Have you ever heard a friend say something like: *"If only I could get my deepest wish fulfilled, then I would be happy"*?

How true do you think that statement is and why?

 ## Historical context

Jesus was extremely controversial in his day. While the common, despised or marginalized people were drawn to him, the religious authorities were frequently incensed by his claims, his associations and his lifestyle.

There were several types of religious leaders in Jesus' day. In this story we are introduced to two significant groups. The Pharisees were a religious sect of Jews who focused on a strict interpretation of the Law of Moses (the first five books of the Bible). The second group, called the teachers of the law (some of whom were also Pharisees), were professionally trained in teaching and applying the law.

We will meet a paralyzed man and his faithful friends, who were so eager for him to be healed of paralysis that they went to where Jesus was teaching in a Galilean town. To their surprise the house was packed not only with local people, but with religious leaders who had traveled from all over the country to listen to this new rabbi who was gaining so much attention. We never learn the paralyzed man's name nor how he developed this condition. Jesus responds to his need in a surprising way.

9

One day Jesus was teaching, and Pharisees and teachers of the law were sitting there. They had come from every village of Galilee and from Judea and Jerusalem. And the power of the Lord was with Jesus to heal the sick. [18] Some men came carrying a paralyzed man on a mat and tried to take him into the house to lay him before Jesus. [19] When they could not find a way to do this because of the crowd, they went up on the roof and lowered him on his mat through the tiles into the middle of the crowd, right in front of Jesus.

[20] When Jesus saw their faith, he said, "Friend, your sins are forgiven."

[21] The Pharisees and the teachers of the law began thinking to themselves, "Who is this fellow who speaks blasphemy? Who can forgive sins but God alone?"

[22] Jesus knew what they were thinking and asked, "Why are you thinking these things in your hearts? [23] Which is easier: to say, 'Your sins are forgiven,' or to say, 'Get up and walk'? [24] But I want you to know that the Son of Man has authority on earth to forgive sins." So he said to the paralyzed man, "I tell you, get up, take your mat and go home." [25] Immediately he stood up in front of them, took what he had been lying on and went home praising God. [26] Everyone was amazed and gave praise to God. They were filled with awe and said, "We have seen remarkable things today."

Jesus is teaching in the region of the Galilee. The distance from Jerusalem (in the south) to the town of Capernaum (in the north where Jesus was based) is 120 miles. It would take a fit person four or five days to walk that distance!

1 Note where these religious authorities came from (v 17). Why do you think some of the Pharisees and teachers of the law decided to travel such distances and all at the same time?

2 Once the men realize they can't get through the door because of the crowd, what alternative plan do they devise and what are the risks involved (v 18-19)?

10

3 What does it say about the paralyzed man and his friends that they were so determined to get to Jesus?

4 What does Jesus see in these men that impresses him (v 20a)?

5 When Jesus says the man's sins are forgiven (v 20b), what do you think the reaction of the paralytic and his friends might have been?

6 Jesus seems to be saying to this man: "If all I do is heal your body, the happiness won't last, because the root of your problem is deeper than your physical condition." What do you think about this?

7 By saying that his sins were forgiven, what did these religious leaders correctly perceive about the controversial claim Jesus was indirectly making (v 21)?

The religious leaders were amazed by Jesus' healing ministry. But they were outraged by his claim to forgive sin, because they knew that was something only God could do. Jesus didn't say to the paralyzed man: "Look, we all blow it. Nobody's perfect, so just take heart in that." Instead, Jesus proclaimed that the sins of the paralyzed man were forgiven, simply because he had pronounced it so! It was an earth-shattering statement that reflected Jesus' identity and mission—which wasn't lost on the Pharisees!

But what Jesus does next shocks them even more. When the Old Testament religious leaders wanted to invoke authority, they would always cite divine (never personal) authority by saying: "Thus says the Lord." The religious leaders believed the worst sin of all was to commit blasphemy—the claim to be God.

8 What authority did Jesus invoke when he spoke to the paralytic (v 24b)?

So, why does this matter?

C. S. Lewis, an Oxford professor and Christian writer who was once a fervent atheist, wrote:

> *"Then comes the real shock. Among the Jews there suddenly turns up a man who goes about talking as if he was God. He claims to forgive sins. He says he always existed. He says he is coming to judge the world at the end of time ... and when you have grasped that, you will see that what this man said was, quite simply, the most shocking thing that has ever been uttered by human lips."*

Why do you think people who reject the controversial claims that Jesus made about his own identity still call him a great teacher and leader?

BIBLE STUDY ANSWERS

1. Jesus had a reputation by now. For so many religious leaders to have come all at the same time and from such distances, this may have been a planned event, perhaps a formal investigation to test his orthodoxy. His popularity and the claims he was making would have alarmed many religious leaders. While the religious leaders recognize a great miracle has been done, they still haven't arrived at any definitive conclusions.

2. Houses usually had flat roofs, often with external staircases leading up to them. Seeing the crowd, the paralytic might have said, "Let's not trouble the Master anymore." One risk might have been that he could have fallen off the mat!

3. Jesus' reputation preceded him and they clearly believed, at the minimum, that he had healing gifts and was a prophet.

4. Jesus was impressed by "their faith" (plural). It is unlikely that it was only the faith of the bearers (Mark says it was four men) carrying him. All of them, the paralytic included, believed that Jesus had the power to heal him.

5. The paralytic and the bearers must have wondered at first if Jesus had misunderstood! However, the words would have been comforting. In Jesus' day, many people falsely believed that disabilities were the result of some unspecified sin in the past, perhaps in that person or in his ancestors—see John 9 v 2, 34.

6. Jesus' proclamation that his sins were forgiven reveals the heart of what Jesus came to do: to deliver us from our moral and spiritual paralysis. While most contemporary seekers do not believe in sin, it's important to ponder the hidden assumption that Jesus is challenging: "If I got my deepest wish, then everything would be OK." If your group wants to know what Jesus means by "sin" then you might say, "The Bible says it's ignoring God by living without any reference to him. It's saying 'I will decide how to run my life—not the one who created me.' Sin is trying to build our identity on something other than God."

7. It is understandable that the religious leaders were upset. They correctly recognized that only God can forgive sin, but they incorrectly assumed that Jesus was guilty of blasphemy. That is why verse 24 is so important.

8. Jesus heals in his own name, which was unheard of! Jesus performs the cure so that they may know that the Son of Man has authority on earth to forgive sins. Perhaps Jesus is saying that on the surface it looks as if healing is the harder thing, when, in fact, to truly release a person from guilt and pronounce a word of divine forgiveness is the harder thing. Either way, Jesus accomplishes both.

So, why does this matter?

This question is aiming to help the group to see that they cannot put Jesus in the category of "good teacher" or "great man"—that he was either God on earth, or a fraud. Of course, it sounds much more polite and acceptable to say Jesus was a great leader rather than explicitly reject him altogether, which is why people attempt to treat him in this way. That is still a rejection though—it is treating Jesus as far less than he claimed to be, a little like treating a spouse as a paid cleaner.

GOODBYE!

REFLECTION: AS YOU FINISH...

1. If you had to sum up in one sentence how this course has changed how you think and feel about evangelism, what would it be?

2. In what ways is the Spirit prompting you to change in some way, in order to share Christ with those around you?

3. What are the biggest dangers that would stop you living out what you've seen in the Bible during these sessions? How will you resist those dangers?

NEXT STEPS

~ Pray about whether there is someone (or some people) you could invite to a Seeker Bible Study. Speak to others in the group to see whether you could form a group with one or two others and their non-Christian friends who would like to come.

PRAY

~ Thank God for what you have learned during this course.

~ Ask God to use you to lead one person to Christ during this year!

~ Ask God to guide you about starting a Seeker Bible Study, and whether you should invite another Christian in your group to lead it with you, so that both of you can bring your friends.

EXTRA
RESOURCES

PRAYING POWERFULLY

God "is able to do immeasurably more than all we ask or imagine, according to his power that is at work within us" (Ephesians 3 v 20-21). So you need to and can pray confidently what Paul did: "that whenever I speak, words may be given me so that I will fearlessly make known the mystery of the gospel, for which I am an ambassador..." (Ephesians 6 v 19-20). Praying powerfully is about praying to our powerful Father in the ways he has taught us to pray in his word.

Which non-Christians has God placed in your life? What is their central interest in life? (For example, sports, family, the arts, education, technology, retirement, business.)

Friends:

Relatives:

Neighbors:

Colleagues:

Ask God to work in them to:

~ create a hunger in them for God.

~ open their eyes to the emptiness of life without him.

~ help them to be aware of their need.

~ open their hearts to be willing to have a spiritual conversation.

~ protect them from the enemy's devices.

~ bless them in specific ways they need.

Ask God to work in you to:

~ help you live a consistent and attractive Christian life.

~ make you a person others want to talk to because of your authenticity.

~ increase your courage and your faith that he will use you just as you are.

BIG QUESTIONS

Week One: Questions about God and Faith

(Select the questions you feel are most appropriate for the person.)

1. When it comes to spiritual matters, would you describe yourself as unconvinced, interested or a believer, and why?

2. Just for the sake of argument—suppose there is a God. What would you want this God to be like?

3. If there is a God and you could ask him one question, what would it be?

4. Does the idea of having faith in a God we can't see strike you as superstitious? Do you think we might operate by "faith" in some areas of our life without realizing it? Do you ever trust in things you can't see or prove?

5. According to the Bible, we all worship something—whether it's God or success or family etc. Do you think that is true? (If they seem open, you might say, "May I share some things I used to put my trust in before becoming a Christian, and still find it easy to put my trust in today?")

Remember to conclude by telling them how much you've enjoyed listening to what they say. Ask if you could meet one more time next week!

Week Two: Questions on the Human Problem and Jesus Christ

1. What do you think is the biggest problem in the world today? What is the solution?
   They will probably say that the problem is either external or internal. If they say the problem is internal (e.g. we are greedy, or selfish) and the solution is external (we need more education) then you might point that out. For example, one Christian using these questions said to their friend, "Hmm, but if, as you say, we are ALL greedy, and the solution is education—then who's going to teach the class?!"

2. Who do you think Jesus really was? What do you base this on?

   If they ask, "But how do we even know that he really lived?" then feel free to say that there is credible historical evidence that backs up his life and claims and the things he is reported to have done. These historical records of course include the Bible, but also Jewish historians like Josephus and Roman historians such as Tacitus.

3. Have you ever read the biblical accounts of the life of Jesus? What did you think? Did it make any sense?

4. Have you ever had an experience in which you felt God was there or making himself known to you?

5. I'm currently doing a course with some friends at my church, and one thing the course presenters encouraged us to do is to ask a friend if we could take a few minutes to share the essence of the Christian message with them. I don't know that I'll be very good at this, but would you be willing to listen, and then give me feedback on where I was clear and what didn't make sense?

HELPFUL WAYS TO OUTLINE THE GOSPEL

Along with the Creation - Crisis - Christ - Commitment - Completion outline given in Talk One in Session Six, there are countless great ways to explain the gospel to someone. Here are just a few, ranging from very simple to more visual:

CHRIST JESUS

The message of Christianity can be summed up by these two names:

"Christ" means God's promised, all-powerful, eternal King. Christ came to show how great it is to be under his perfect, loving rule—but the fact that there is a Christ is concerning, for none of us have lived under his rule, preferring to rule ourselves. Christ will rule his perfect kingdom forever, but we face being excluded from it because we have rejected him.

But...

"Jesus" means God rescues. Christ did not come only to show his kingdom, but to open his kingdom. He died and rose again so that we can be forgiven and restored to relationship with him, living under his rule. He rescues us from exclusion from his kingdom, and to enjoy his kingdom with him forever.

So to come into his kingdom, all we need to do is recognize him as Christ—our King, who is to be in charge of our lives—and to trust him as Jesus—our God-sent rescuer, who forgives and restores us.

DO / DONE

This outline can be done with a scrap of paper or a napkin:

Write "DO": There's no doubt that there is something wrong with the world—just look around you. Humans are not in good relationship with each other, with the world, or most importantly of all, with God.

All world religions seek to confront that problem, and they can all be summed up in two letters—"DO." They teach what we must "DO" to be restored to relationship with God. But the problem is that we can never know if we are doing the right things, or enough of the right things—and in fact the Bible says that "all have sinned and fall short of the glory of God" (Romans 3 v 23). We can never DO enough.

But the message of Christianity is uniquely different. It is summed up by four letters: "DONE." Christianity teaches that what we could not do, God has done for us, by sending Jesus, his Son. Jesus lived a perfect life, and then he died to take the punishment for all our sin—our rejection of God and his rule. "God demonstrates his own love for us in this: while we were still sinners, Christ died for us" (Romans 5 v 8). So to be restored to eternal relationship with God, we need to stop trying to DO good things to earn it, and simply trust that Jesus has DONE all we need to enjoy it.

THE BARRIER BROKEN

GOD

HUMANS

"God saw all that he had made, and it was very good."

Genesis 1 v 31

God made people to enjoy perfect life in his world, in relationship with him, under his loving rule, forever.

GOD

HUMANS

"All have sinned and fall short of the glory of God." *Romans 3 v 23*
We reject God's loving rule—we sin. This means we don't know God and are separated from enjoying perfect life with him, now and in the future.

GOD

J

HUMANS

"The Word was God ... The Word became flesh and made his dwelling among us." *John 1 v 1, 14*
Jesus Christ lived on earth as a man. He is the "Word"—God's Son, who has always lived under his Father's loving rule. He reveals to us what God is like and shows how great life in relationship with God is.

GOD

HUMANS

"Christ ... suffered once for sins, the righteous for the unrighteous, to bring you to God."   *1 Peter 3 v 18*

Jesus died on a cross. He took the punishment of separation from God that we deserve as sinful ("unrighteous") people, so that he can give us a right relationship with God.

GOD

HUMANS

"God has raised this Jesus to life ... he has received from the Father the promised Holy Spirit and has poured [him] out."   *Acts 2 v 32-33*

God raised his Son, Jesus, back to life. He returned to heaven and sent his Spirit into the world, to enable people to know him and live under his loving rule.

GOD

HUMANS

"Serve the living and true God, and ... wait for his Son from heaven ... Jesus, who rescues us from the coming wrath."   *1 Thessalonians 1 v 9-10*

Christians are people who:

· *turn* away from rejecting God's loving rule, and try to serve him.

· *wait* for his Son to return, to remake and rule the world so that it's perfect again.

· *know* they will not face God's anger at their sin (his "wrath"), because Jesus has rescued them by being punished in their place on the cross.

Other great gospel explanations can be found online at:

evangelism.intervarsity.org/how/gospel-outline/big-story-tutorial-video

navigators.org/Tools/Evangelism%20Resources/Tools/The%20Bridge%20to%20Life

APOLOGETICS: RESOURCES FOR ANSWERING TOUGH QUESTIONS

General
Books:
The Reason for God (Tim Keller)
If You Could Ask God One Question (Paul Williams and Barry Cooper)
Hope Has Its Reasons (Rebecca Manley Pippert)
What Kind of God? (Michael Ots)
Fool's Talk (Os Guinness)
Can Man Live Without God? (Ravi Zacharias)
The Twilight of Atheism (Alister McGrath)

Something short:
Good Question (Carl Laferton)

Online:
bethinking.org
christianityexplored.org/tough-questions
rzim.org/just-thinking-broadcasts

The Reliability of the Bible
Why Trust the Bible? (Amy Orr-Ewing)
Can We Really Trust the Bible? (Barry Cooper)
Is God a Moral Monster? (Paul Copan)

Science and Faith
God's Undertaker (John Lennox)
Unnatural Enemies (Kirsty Birkett)
Who Made God? (Edgar Andrews)

Sexual Ethics
Is God Anti-Gay? (Sam Allberry)

What is the Meaning of Sex? (Denny Burk)

The Problem of Suffering and Evil
Unspeakable (Os Guinness)
If I Were God, I'd End all the Pain (John Dickson)
Why Suffering? (Ravi Zacharias and Vince Vitale)
Why? (Sharon Dirckx)

The Resurrection
The Case for Christ (Lee Strobel)
Raised? (Jonathan Dodson)

Other Religions
Jesus Among Other Gods (Ravi Zacharias)
Seeking Allah, Finding Jesus (Nabeel Qureshi)
No God But One (Nabeel Qureshi)
If I were God, I'd Make Myself Clearer (John Dickson)

Intolerance
Is the Bible Intolerant? (Amy Orr-Ewing)
The Intolerance of Tolerance (Don Carson)

Relativism and Truth
True for You, but not for Me (Paul Copan)

Worldview
Naming the Elephant (James Sire)
The Universe Next Door (James Sire)
What's Your Worldview? (James Anderson)

Becky Pippert
MINISTRIES

Becky's years of experience of talking to people about Jesus shine through on each page of these Bible studies, written for Christians to walk through with their non-Christian friends. These "Seeker Bible Studies" have proven incredibly effective in bringing people around the world to see who Jesus is, and what he is offering to them.

Uncovering the Life of Jesus contains six studies in the Gospel of Luke. *Discovering the Real Jesus* comprises seven encounters with Jesus from John's Gospel.

thegoodbook.com | thegoodbook.co.uk | thegoodbook.com.au